*To some of the most ardent supporters
of my student career: my teachers.
Thank you for everything.
N.S.*

As I Pass.

I've heard that when you pass,
your life flashes before your eyes.
I should hope that it will be like a vintage
movie
where I will see the Clark to my Grace or
the Noah to my Allie.
A reel of film
developed carefully, caressed only by my
loving arms and witnessed only by me.
At last, one secret
I will never share.
Until death do us part,
I bid you adieu.

Cabernet.

I said I was ok, and I lied.

Lies make me hurt inside,
a sharp pain reminiscent of
my painful days.

She said I was weak, I listened.
I couldn't stop, so I did it in secret.

God will send me to hell for I have sinned,
I have told a lie to keep myself afloat.

There are no exceptions to this rule,
she told me.

You are a victim of your own soliloquy.

I will not be present at your pity party.

I sip my wine and collapse into it.

Blackout.

Playing my music made them mad.
They tried to put handcuffs on me.
I didn't like that.
I hit them. Then I went to jail.
And they locked me up.
Made me promise I never play my guitar on
the street again.
I only play it here.

Pressure.

How the urge could madly lather
It dreamed of crushing all
but one girl.
It lived in her light.
He wants it because
beauty is pounding in his ugly mist.

Why?

Light swims
Asking, pleading
Why was my dream death?

Nobody would listen.
Soon Light faded.

Dull and gone forever.
Light is not beautiful anymore.
Greed consumes Dark.
He wants her light.

He traps her with his cloak
Black mist surrounds her. Help! She cries
Help does not listen.

Dark is now light.
Light is now dark.
Dark consumes light.
Light consumes dark.

What a travesty!
They cry.

For our light is now dark and our dark is
now light.

The glimmer that blankets the earth during
the day is faded.

The starry light is now gone.

The romantic pitch-black nights are dead.

But Light is okay being dark,
and Dark is okay being light.

Window.

The sky is blue.
Not the strangely peculiar shade of blue
whose waves lap against the sand.
Not the blue of sickening sadness or gut-
wrenching heartbreak.
Not the tinkling blue of an antiquated piano
that you found for $200 at the thrift store.
The blue of joy, of memories, of hope, of
peace.
With the cotton candy clouds woven into
shapes unrecognizable to some, but fields of
imagination for others.

Run.

The effervescent smile of the sky
The golden sunshine bright
The maiden runs with wild eyes
Hair blowing in the wind
She twirls along with the bees,
flower blooming beside her feet.

Stop.

I'm not going to say that I have
always wanted to keep going
despite the fact that I've been
excellent about wearing a mask
that is wonderful at captivating
others so long
as it lets me cry in peace.

My eyes are now red and my
cheeks remain ashen,
but my face is a rubicund, radiant
thing that is enough to throw
people off.

Hypocrisy.

I am often told that I am too white to be
brown
or too brown to be white.

I am too ugly to be pretty but too pretty to
be ugly.

I am too intelligent to be average but too
average to be intelligent.

I am too existent to be nonexistent but too
nonexistent to be existent.

Waiving.

I'm waiving my waving,
I'm sick of it now.
I'm waiving my waving,
Still not quite sure how.
I cannot stand waving, at everyone else,
especially when they make me clean up their
mess.
I stare out the window, fingers clamped,
gentle wrist,
I'm waiving my waving,
for that's what I wish.

Listen.

Hear the birds whisper on the branch that is
chestnut brown.
The *whoosh* of the spring wind.
Hear the blackbird's croak and the
nightingale's song echoing from far away.
The burning, crackling fireplace.
Beware, do listen.
Perfection is not eternal.

One Wish.

I wish the sky was crisp and blue
The rainbows stretched from each corner.
The clouds spun from cotton candy,
when people said "fine and dandy".
I wish we didn't have cars
And only good weather, permitting
I only wish to reach for the stars
But it seems the past is more fitting.

Memory.

I remember for a second
to feel disgust and ignorance
but now even the bad things've left me
and I'm stuck in the losing bid.
I want to feel something else now
something good or something bad
but I know I can't so let me relive my past
and feebly attempt to feel sad.

It's just a blood curdling anger
or a nanosecond where I
lose my temper too much.
It's mostly blips of sadness
and attempting to remember
your touch.

I can't feel anything at all
hearing those wretched words
echoing in the hall
I can't see everything I'd seen
hearing voices laughing telling me
what I'd once been.

Shtum.

"I walked to school, 4 miles each day,
I fell sick and couldn't go home,
I shared a mattress with my 6 siblings,
My mother's jewels reduced to none."
What did I have, that made me worthy?
Permitted me to boast about my journey?
They said I played the victim card,
undeserving of pity unlike them. Psychology
is overrated, they said,
physical exhaustion a greater cause.
Not once did I ever shed a tear,
instead I hoped I would feel pain I couldn't
bear.
Feelings are real, not fake, not weak,
they create the beauty for which we seek.
I have yet to feel pain, or "no sorrow no
gain",
for everything was handed to me on a silver
platter.

The Price.

My feet were bruised, and bloody too,
the tendons bent out of shape.
The pain was suddenly too much for me to
bear,
but I knew I would have felt it anyways.
Pain is inevitable, if you do what you love,
ancient tales spoke firmly.
I don't want to feel this anymore,
but I will do it anyway, I say.
If I had stuck with my mother-art,
not gone to this foreign fragility,
I would be better of by now, I assure,
but time is what time can be.

The Truth.

Society is a necessary evil.
When we suffer, our chaos is heightened.

For if our intentions were clear,
implicitly obeyed, then
we would need no other reason,
making necessary a surrender, unanimous,
for the well-being of the rest.

Security seems to to be the real end,
as it conveniently appears most preferable to
everyone else.

Imposter.

I knew they were lies, gleaming and white,
spilling from in between her teeth.
Her stories spun with golden thread,
too ridiculous to believe.
I was sick of the lies, but I let them go on,
because I was afraid of losing it all.
But lies aren't the foundation of a stable house,
instead they will make it all crumble.

Again.

You too? I thought you were different.
That's what I say to myself to justify the fact
that I trusted them before you.
I gave you my all, held no standard
against you.
Both of you, you liars.
You said I was your friend.
Held a knife to each other's throats
but you stabbed me instead.

Ego.

Just let me be. Stop hurting me.
Your voice means nothing but the world to
me.
I hate to admit how much you've done,
you scoundrel, with scheming hugs.
You've robbed me of my right to choose,
blackmailed me into going screw-loose.
You've dangled it all, but snatched it away,
done nothing but lie, anyways.
My relationships are built on trust, not lies,
like yours,
but the difference is, the lies seeped through
your pores.
I've given you more than a thousand
chances,
but everything you say puts me in trances.
I've overthought every statement you've
said,
studied your body language out of pure
dread.
I wish I could tell you how much I hate you,
but my ego won't let me get to a
breakthrough.

Mistaken.

We were told we were endowed with certain
unalienable rights,
there is proof that they were not amended.
This isn't a home, nor a country without,
the lives of the people being paramount.
So when you choke the life out of an
innocent human, a sickening grin spreading
on your face,
remember clearly, that those rights didn't
disappear, just because you felt a certain
way. Their parents, who loved and raised
them, the siblings with which they fought.
Their friends, who were rocks to lean on,
didn't imagine their love would be gone.
Did they deserve this death? ask closely,
Did they think this day would be their last?
It is unfathomable the number it would take,
for a finger to move on Capitol Hill.

Assured.

Why is it that they,
who have done nothing at all,
mingle with everyone,
the tallest of all?

Why is it that I,
who have done everything in my power
to attempt to shower
myself in words louder and prouder
am told I cannot sit with those
at that table, instead
I will have to eat at my own stable?

Why is it that I,
who am clearly more deserving,
who carries the weight of a family,
on my knees am left helpless,
instead I'm not hopeless,
in good stead I will find
the strength I need to make sure
they are breathless.

Bye?

Please remember me, and all the times we
had,
I know this isn't the best thing to ask.
I've been told to forget you, unfriend you,
but that thought fills my heart with dread.
Too many times you have given me sorrow,
toyed with my heart strings every day.
I really don't care if I hate you,
please just reach out to me anyway.
I've scoured my photos and found you,
reread texts and listened to recordings.
I know that I was "dry" as they say,
but my ego inside kept on throbbing.
I still hope you'll call me once more,
although I don't seek another wish.
I hope you know how much you hurt me,
I hope you know all that you'll miss.

Is it because you told me too much?
Or is it the lies that you crafted?
I'll never know the myriad of reasons,
that caused you to whisper goodbyes.

Torture.

You stare at me plainly, yet act with
indifference.
I gave you a million chances, but you left
nonetheless.
I'm done playing games, done heeding your
lies,
acting less than my best to please you.
I met you and they told me, your ways were
trouble at once,
I chose to go against their wishes.
Alas, now I know,
as their sayings all told,
you were nothing but torture to me.
I spoke of you always,
I thought of you for days,
I hoped that you felt the same way.
You told me you placed in my trust your
life,
and like a blithering fool, I believed you.
You've found another one, I'm sure, to lie
to,
I feel no remorse, but pure hatred, I lie for
you,
you've slipped from my life,
I've forgotten all about you,

all I ever wanted to say is here, staring at
you.
You've made me feel lower than I've ever
been,
told me every time that I'd committed a sin.
The only bad choice I've made till date,
was letting your problems overcrowd my
plate.

Betrayal.

I don't know how else to begin,
in expressing my anger and regret.
I don't know how else to tell you, you've
made my life begin to drift.
You've caused my problems, anguish and
pain,
you've stolen my happiness,
from this I have nothing to gain.
I regret every moment I spent, waiting for
you to respond.
Proofreading my messages that I sent,
wondering where you'd gone.
Silence is the greatest form of betrayal,
about that I am extremely sure,
for if I meant something to you,
I surely would have gotten more.
I've cried myself to sleep,
because you showed me who I was,
not a picture perfect prom queen,
but an angry, malicious "whore".

I still see you every week,
and the revenge which I'll seek,
is leaving you to rot,
alone, in your cot.

You've made me hate myself,
and the morals for which I stand.
I've sacrificed morning and night, just to
hear your rants.

I can do nothing but scream now,
as the damage is already done- you put me
on a pedestal,
then reduced me to none.

I seek.

Why am I not good enough? Or pretty? Or
sweet?
Why can't I be the one with pearly white
teeth?
I don't wear bikinis,
or shop with my "crew".

I don't have friends, like the ones they do.
They're there for each other,
they love one another so,
they're given everything and more,
rock-solid to each other, like earth's core.

It isn't fair, how they do everything,
put on a pedestal without doing anything.
It's nothing else but my attitude, I think,
and until someone says no,
that's what it'll be.

Nostalgia.

I miss those days, skies blue and clear,
we'd drive with the windows down.
The outside hot enough to sear,
blasting music, killing our ears.
We'd stop at gas stations, and eat fast food,
drive up to the city,
the scene from a book,
and the song from the movie.
My hair in a yellow bandanna,
we'd dream about the end, like our nanas.
I miss your jeep, with replaced tires,
the car freshener that smelled like bananas,
I'll miss eating cupcakes in the backseat,
and falling asleep while you drove at the
wheel.
I'll miss it more than you'll ever know, even
more than your graduation bow.

Tepid.

Tepid is my coffee, not hot like I wish.
Tepid is the room, not warm, not cold.
Tepid is my mood, not sorrow or gloom.
Tepid are my friends, not few, not many.
Tepid is the water, with which I take a bath.
Tepid is the sweat, of the hand with which I
bash.

Seams.

I am so excited I rip the hanger off
the cold, metallic rod.
I unzip the dress and lay it out on my bed.
It is beautiful, pink and gold,
a reminder of my heritage.
I strip eagerly, feeling my cold hands
against my coarse skin.
I slide into the skirt and tie it on the side,
it is turquoise and resplendent.
The blouse, I unhook from each of the
sides, and slide it onto my arms.
I cannot move them around, I cry in dismay,
attempting to squeeze myself into the front.
It does not fit, I am desolate,
I have no other one.

Luxury.

I have no luxury, none of any kind,
I'm surrounded in splendor, with nowhere to
hide.
Gold ready at my beckon,
silver ladles at my wish,
yet I envy those who wash my dish.
Their mothers fondle them,
their fathers give them kisses,
all while their siblings share spare mittens.
They are unfortunate, as many would say,
but their heart, oh their heart,
is more than mine any day.
Yes, they scour pans, scrape grime off the
walls,
but even their parents answer their calls.

Convivial.

We sat around the table,
wine in stemmed glasses.
We toast to new beginnings, and old bursts
of compassion.
We reminisce over memories, recollect past
flings.
We fail to appreciate,
our feelings and our things.
We were all convivial, considered being
social trivial.
Yet those feelings in our hearts, made it all
the more difficult to part.

Contuse.

I have no bruises seen,
nor scars to remind me either.
No proof of what I dealt with, nothing
tangible of the latter.
You haven't made me bleed, but you've also
contused me.
Not medically, perhaps,
but mentally I've collapsed.
The bruises dark and ugly,
I cannot convalesce.
They aren't there for them to see,
but they're only there for me.

Mommy.

Mommy, please, listen to me,
your praise means more than three worlds to
me.
Your past is glittery, elusive, and dark,
you're the celebrity of my heart.
Mommy, please, don't use those words,
"slut" and "fat" and "fuck you, ungrateful
girl".
Mommy, please, I implore you to
understand,
for you've been there everywhere to hold
my hand.

Voices.

The yelling needed to stop,
I knew it and took essence.
It was enough to pretend to have talk-shows
in my bed.
I start out small,
but my problems get corpulent, they
consume me,
feeding off of my sadness. And my tears.
They lick them up, like cats drinking milk.

The Vent.

Not white, but a rather peculiar shade of
cream.
Its eyes bore holes through me.
The crevices dusty,
paint chipping,
silent, but loud.
It whooshes.

Golden.

Treat them with kindness, they say, but it's
different.
I did, and it worked, minutes until it didn't.
Then I ceased, and held,
but magically it did.
I'm starting to think
I care more than I should.

Bimetallic.

I've developed more of an emotional connection to my heater than to my friends.

It is always warm, never cold or cunning, and comforts me when I am harmed.

I set it at seventy-two, mode one to be exact.

I sit in front of a bonfire, with a knapsack on my back.

Goodbye.

I wasn't there when she passed.
The next minute I was on an airplane,
soaring in the sky,
much akin to the way I hoped she was in
heaven.
I didn't know her too well,
but she made them cry.
Their walls were broken,
on the day that she died.
Her picture was hung, on the cream colored
walls,
and in that moment, I knew,
the feeling of lucidity. .
Her thoughts, filled her head,
like mine did now.
Her feelings vibrant,
so were mine.
I see her floating down in a parachute,
then open my eyes, alas.
It was a dream, like much of good that
occurs.
A dream, not a moment, etched in time.
On occasions, she floats down to say hello.
I wish I could have said goodbye.

Critiques.

Please tell me what she did that I didn't,
I desperately want to know.
Your words meant everything to me,
I guess you could say I loved you like a
sister.
I know I'm 10 times better,
at least that's what they say.
Yet I don't know if I am enough,
not just for you but for everyone else too. I
rest all of my faith in one moment, but it
seems as though
that one moment isn't enough.
For you, or for anyone.

Worldly.

Eyes are an abyss,
black as the night.

Lashes the mossy rocks coating
the beach side.

Brows the sand,
microscopically imperfect.

Eyelids the folds in the ocean, the waves,
cheekbones the sculpted walls of rock.

Lips the fruit of trees in a dreamy orchard,
nose the mountains made from God's hands.

Bow from its father, the one and only Cupid,
forehead the flat grasslands and prairies.

Jaw the borders between ocean and land,
teeth the icebergs, deathly and gorgeous.

Tongue of a dragon, slit in the middle.

Saved it.

I wish to cry, but the tears won't come.
When they do, they come at the most
horrific moments. The saddest feeling being
holding back tears, glimmering like the sun
and stars.
When they don't, it is almost karmic in a
way, "gave you a chance but you didn't take
it".
They flow like silver down my cheeks,
they glimmer in the light of the moon.
I huddle under the covers, praying they
won't be heard. I smile in the mirror,
praying they won't be seen.
I dance in the shadows, praying they won't
come. But they do.

Perfect.

The perfect day would be something out of a
book.
I'd awaken at dawn,
and hear the birds chirp as the golden rays
spread across the sky.
The cushy duvet would wrap me,
a swath of warm hugs, like a child.
Everything would clean itself,
the coffee pot would magically run,
the scent of candles would fill the air. Utopia
is a funny thing,
that morning will never exist.

Empty.

I am empty.
The can of feelings has run dry.
Each second has me feeling something else,
an inconvenience, if you ask me.
The mood ring would likely explode
at the rate at which I feel things.
My thoughts fill a cavern,
bleak, cold, and snowy.
On top of a hill.
My hands are stiff and cold,
my hair is messy.
I am empty.
I am empty.
I am empty.

Bell.

You know who you are if you remember our conversation.

Perhaps I want to look you in the eye one final time, to whisper *checkmate*.

I did what you told me you'd lose respect for me if I did.

It's a wonderful feeling, not giving a shit.

I truly enjoy it.

Yet I did you a favor, a solid, even though I hated you-

I loved you enough to leave myself.

I hated myself enough to love you.

War.

I am too young they say,
too immature to understand,
to comprehend the full extent
of the problems in this land.

I am too brown to have an opinion
on topics that don't concern me
because I am not truly American.

I am too womanly to know
the pain that they go through
my job is to sit and listen.

Yet rooted deep, like the roots of a tree,
I stand ready to swallow my pride.

No more, I say, this is a systemic problem,
I am more than enough in the end of the
bargain!

I will brandish my sword with an oath of
fortitude and assume my seat as the
commander-in-chief.

Bath.

I entered the shower, feeling the steamy hot water encase my skin with an invisible shield.

 I scrubbed myself vigorously until the skin on my calves began to slightly peel and my callused feet began to turn red once more.

I needed to clean my brain, too.

Bye.

I guess I've always wondered what death feels like. Voluntary death, I suppose.

What's so beautiful about it is that your life truly remains in your hands.

Metaphorically and literally.

At times I've vehemently felt the need to let someone know my wrath, my worth, the importance of me as a person, but I see now that it isn't necessary.

Perhaps a small bit of myself wants you to miss me.

I want you to regret those words "don't take someone for granted." I know you did.

I know you would think I would never do what you perceived as the ultimate act of cowardice.

I did.

In Love?

Am I in love?
The sound of your name
is enough to make me blush.
The way your eyes dance,
I can see each difference in you.
I can't see flaws, however.
I guess some people were created to be
perfect.
Breathtaking.
Like you.

Unfair.

I'd never felt disgust at my body until that
day.
"Sweetheart" and "darling"
he cooed.
It had never occurred to me
that my breasts could be
"vulgar".
All my life I saw
large "lady parts"
was key in making a man swoon.
My legs needed to be sticks.
My derrière needed to be plump.
Yet when I had all that,
the curves,
the breasts,
when I wore those godforsaken shorts.
He called me darling.
And stared at my ass the whole walk down
the hall.

Cold.

I wasn't created to be mean.
A concept that seemed so foreign, difficult
to grasp.
I enjoy helping people.
I cannot manipulate.
I am not a sword, like you,
I do not wish to do things
for the sake of receiving something.
I am just plain nice,
the advantageous see me
as a prime opportunity
to carry out their wicked plans.
But I am not gullible,
I am cold.
I am cold, but nice.
Am I allowed to be?
Feelings are confusing,
they rebel against each other,
like oil and water.

Hourglass.

I love to obsess
until my hair falls out and
my skin becomes pale.

Stuck.

I am trapped,
in this place I call home.
I am imprisoned
with many others.
I am stuck and I cannot get out, but if I can,
I cannot leave without my mask.
When I get home, I take it off, but I put on
another one.
I wish I could traverse the closet of masks,
that I subject myself to on the daily.

Secret.

I have a secret.
I will share it,
just as I am baring my heart,
my thoughts,
the vast expanse of a realm that is
my emotions.
I hate being judged.
I despise judging others.
Yet if life didn't judge me so harshly,
this endeavor wouldn't have existed.
I do things out of the fear of not doing
enough. I am scared,
tired,
hurting,
behind a mask.

Because.

You don't know me.
I don't know myself.
From the discussions I've had,
I have put myself at a problematic place.
I don't know who I am,
or what I like to do.
I don't know why or how
I do things.
I learn, do, listen,
because everyone does so.
Yet to write, becomes my release.
I finally know what I love to do,
I can explore the uncharted territory
knowing that I have explored and conquered
my own land.
My new home.
Where I wholly, truly, and amply exist,
in every way, shape, and form.

Succumb.

I rest my head against the pillow wishing I
could control my thoughts like I do the
television.
I like to control everything I can,
so when I cannot,
I succumb.
I am rather powerless in the realm of
dreams,
the monarchs wield their staffs, but I do not.
They control me, their little puppet.
I am powerless, voiceless,
and trapped.
I am shaken awake in the wee hours of the
morning,
suffocating against my pillow.
I see my subconscious moments before I
awaken,
and in those glorious moments,

I see my thoughts entwine with my
nightmares.
Yet just as I am about to reach the climax,
the lightning bolts rush.
The dream is gone,
and I am the monarch once again.

You came.

Where did you go?
Forgive my incessant questions,
but I thought we were friends.
You told me you trusted me with your life,
yet you retracted as though I was the devil.

Throughout our friendship, you weren't the
best, either.
You were conniving, and malicious,
but maintained this pretentious mask.

You begged for pity, which I gave to you.
I would reread our conversations for hours
just to see if it was something I'd said.

So was it?

You keep behaving as though everything is
fine, but it isn't.
Not in my head, at least.
Even though I'm the kind to overthink and
over critique my every move, or in this case,
my every message.

Just shoot me a message and let me know
why you dangled it all in front of me, then
snatched it away.

It would mean the world if you told me why
you said goodbye.

Maybe then, I'd lay my thoughts to rest.

I know this is a part of your master plan to
drive me to self-destruct,
but I am stronger than your lies.

But I left.

I don't want to leave.
Not now, not ever.
I am rooted, like a graceful willow tree,
to this place I can call home.
I will never leave, because
my love for my homeland
and my love for its plethora
of people,
of hope,
will trump any and all
hatred towards it.
It has survived the wrongful invasion
of numerous people.
We celebrate their inventions,
yet we know they are ours.
Like siblings, yet on battleground,
but this time,
what we had will never come back.
It has taken years of suffering,
of wrongful decisions,
of power-hungry rule,
for us to realize that we are one.
We all sit under the same beach umbrella,
and share our snacks, memories, and things
all the way around.

Teflon.

I see her twirling, carefree,
her onyx-colored hair flanking her carnation
colored cheeks.
I see her doe-like eyes,
and stare into them,
afraid to fall down the abyss.
I see her and everything she did, how it
triumphs anything I can ever do. For she has
survived and still manages to crack a smile.
She loves me even though she knows that I
will never be as talented,
as beautiful, inside and out,
as she is.

Lucid.

I enter the room
purple lights flash around.
Highlighter yellow glow sticks
are around people's necks.
It reeks of vodka
and bubblegum.
Music blasts from the secondhand speakers
the surfaces like the
millions of eyes of flies.
I sip my drink
and enter a kaleidoscope.
Orange, hot pink
and cyan cloud me.
There he is.
Glitter showers from the sky,
but I cannot seem to find the ground.
A pit of black encases me.
He stands,
like a don
holding a gun to my forehead.
The electric blue lights flash
but I don't know where from.
His army arises from the shadows,
bearing gifts.

"Dance with me"
he says,
a wicked grin spreading across his face.
"NO"
I vehemently shake my head,
or what's left of it.
He grasps my wrist and turns it blue and
purple and green and yellow
and orange and pink and dances.
With me.
I scream and shout but there isn't a speaker
on the wall. Almost as if it is my worst
nightmare or my best dream.
Until I am sucker-punched back to reality,
by the caterwaul of a siren.

Implicit.

Why don't you trust me?
I trust you implicitly.
So much so that I will back you to the hilt
even when you are wrong.
So when you say you do not trust me despite
knowing I am not like them I am hurt,
angered, and enraged.
I am not like you
I will never be like you
but I want to be like you.
All I've ever wanted
was to make my own decisions about me.
You do not "own me"
as you say
I own myself.
I am free, but wrongfully in shackles.
They will never go away,
like my pain.

Lies.

My pain has not gone,
like you said it would.
It is still there,
raw as ever.
Liar, liar, liar, liar, liar.
I can feel him
staring yet once again.
You arrogant, ignorant, liar.
I feel my shame
multiply and divide
until it spreads all over my body. I feel pain,
you pusillanimous, dastardly liar.
I feel their judgemental eyes
as if it was my fault.
My shorts were too short
or my hair was too long
or my eyes were too dark
or my feet were too dainty.
My gaze led him on
and I wouldn't be surprised if they said my
voice did too.
You sick, twisted liar.

Cheater.

You were my savior, your patience
let me open my heart to you

and you broke it so I'm never
going trust another man ever again.

You were my treasure, guilty pleasure,
and i thought i was yours until I walked in

and found you already replacing me,
and I vowed, I'd never
never trust a man again

'till the day that I die.

Already.

You said that you'd miss me
the day you went on that trip.
I stared at my finger and
whispered I'd miss you again.

I thought you would be back
and I would lay in your chest,
but you didn't call back-
you left on the day that I did

And you said you'd be with me,
'rich and through poor' you'd see
I wouldn't try to be
yours I would leave you but you've already

Alone.

Why did you lie?
Why did you try
to leave me just like her?
I never asked for anything,
not even a word.
I met you that Monday,
made them sit in the cold.
We snickered, and laughed,
I thought it would never get old.
This was the second one,
where I said I would forgive,
and forgive was everything less than what I
did.
I sat through your calls,
texted you immediately when you asked,
and yet it never took time for me.
Forgive me if I've done anything wrong,
but I can do nothing but stare hopelessly.

Empress.

I figured that
if I got used to it enough,
maybe it wouldn't bother me.
But since it is
arguably the largest organ
my skin hurts more than my heart.
Can I die?
I would rather do so than stare
in the mirror one last time, longing for
beauty.
The lights in my room flicker.
I reach for the disinfectant.
As if spraying my mirror would make my
body seem any less dirty.
It is invisible, the grime.
The filth swallows me whole.
The grease cakes and the
dust sags beneath my eyes.
For a moment, I feel like a queen.
Reigning over a kingdom.
A kingdom of filth.
Like me.

Maybe?

I like you.
This sensation of peculiarity comes over me.
 I like you.
I am scared to say it out loud.
I don't like you.
That sounds much better.
I like my thought of you, maybe.
Perhaps it is all too clear in my head.
I cannot like you.
I cannot bear another heartbreak.
If friendship was hard,
then love must be impossible.
I know I must not like you.
I cannot like you.
They won't let me like you.
I am scared.
But maybe, like the ancient princes
you will come,
knocking at my door.
To declare your love for me.

It's Open.

Is it odd that I can hear your voice in my
head?
I didn't hear it until a few days ago.
I synthesized distorted videos
and thought it would make my image of you
whole.
Maybe you knew me before I met you,
 maybe this life itself is a sham.
Perhaps I'm not meant to be on this earth,
but of course, as usual, I am.
It rings over and over
and over
and over
until I cringe at my past memories.
I still scroll by your page,
and it leaves me in a daze, so,
what have I done to deserve this?

Corpus.

I hate my body.
Its rolls and curves.
I hate how it doesn't cinch like everyone
else's.
I hate my bosom,
middle-sized,
like the center section in a venn-diagram.
I hate my eyebrows, thick, like bushes,
my nose is too flat,
my forehead is too wide.
My thighs are too thick,
my calves are too big,
my arms are like skewers coated in meat.
My derriere is nonexistent,
my feet are too large,
I'm too short to ever walk the runway.
My face is too pudgy,
my teeth are too uneven,
I'll never be good enough anyways.

Who I am.

The sky is gloomy aquamarine,
her skin glows with dewdrops
from the showers of the night before.

She is I, I am her, she is me.

Her face is smooth,
her forehead alabaster,
her eyes glow with a warm fire,
her lips are rosebuds in a bush of thorns.

She is I, I am her, she is me.

She drives to the pool,
in her run-down Honda,
and sits by the bank this gloomy day.

She is I, I am her, she is me.

Her face in her palms, she weeps till the sun
sets one last time.

She is I, I am her, she is me.

With a heaving sigh,
she wipes them away,
gets back in her car,
drives back to the place where the dew
makes her skin glow.

She is I, I am her, she is me.

Crossroad.

All I have ever wanted
is a family, like theirs.

Don't perceive my words inadequately,
for I love my nest dearly.

I want the squabbles and bustle,
of a community.

I find this more in strangers
than I do in them.

I cannot forgive them for their hurt,
nor the pain or suffering they've caused.

But I love them dearly?

I see now why it is hard
when discussing matters of the heart.

Egg.

Do you know why I always wore skirts?
I was not a woman otherwise.
Do you know why I always stayed silent?
I was not a lady otherwise.
Do you know why I never sat,
with my legs uncrossed,
a gap between them?
I was not feminine otherwise.
Why are you allowed to wear what you
please?
Why can you speak without
begging on your knees?
Why can you sit any way you'd like
and not fear chiding remarks from your
mother?
Such are the questions a sapling
would ask its photosynthesizing mother.
But the sapling will grow
and soon come to know
that it is not a matter of water.

Jealous.

I'll save the introduction because you know
who you are.

You are the envy
of every girl ever to exist.

You are capable, gorgeous, and
a social butterfly.

You are the bane of every
loser-like child's existence.

You are the bane of me.

You can kiss in the hallway
but study so hard.

"She's the kind that will do something"
they say to me.

I, instead, will stare in the mirror
until my jaw gapes in horror and
my eyes fill with dread.

Robber.

You cannot take from me
what I have never had
because if I had it
then you would be greedy.

If I could choose what I wanted
it would be to have something you didn't.
This life of ours sets us in the same mold,
but I'm different from you,
or so I am told.

Reminder.

I can feel your eyes on me.

Silently judging my body.

I can hear your breath,
heavy in the air.

I can feel your sadness.
I am not as perfect as you envisioned.

Yet how is it you thought I was
perfect enough to come look at for a while?

I can smell your hatred.

Don't worry, I hate me too.

Young'un.

We are told from a tender age
not to show who we are, engage
with others like we were to do
in a professional setting when we are two.

We are told of old fables
where our mouths run amuck
and our dreams left to be sown
by the old farmer's luck

We are shown examples of
what are seemingly small infractions
and are constantly reminded of the pain
it takes in raising us.

We are shoved and stepped over
told off with scathing words under
this guise of "humor" and understand not
this world.

We are told to let our guard down
but have we one is the question
for the real ask at hand
is where we are given this suggestion.

Me.

I had never thought my person
would be an adequate justification
for the hatred of this nation
but it is, let me say it.

I had pictured a different life from this
where I would stand aside those hills
but here I am, steadily impaired
by the olive brown color of my skin.

I have been told that I am too pretty
to succeed or to be witty
yet when I am judged by the prettiest
I am too ugly, they bewitch me.

I have been told that this is a freedom,
where my words will not be judged,
yet every single time I open my mouth
the sound of regret flows out.

I have been shown the paragons of success,
yet am defunct in my own bravery,
for I am told that I am not enough,
and my words will still fail me.

My skin is the reason to suppress,
my body the way they oppress me
because I am not the perfect woman
I am as strong and smart as I should be.

I abhor the whole idea of my dress
giving them reasons to address
why I am not as smart or necessary
as they deem me to be.

I will cash my check of gratitude
at the bank I call home,
I am thankful for this experience,
this idea that I am none.

My intelligence is null and void,
my expressions are the reason
the toil of those before me
hasn't emerged victorious,
I am regretful.

They have stood outside the buildings
waiting to come here and yet
they are denied an opportunity
because of the color of their skin.

Your opinions will not crush me
under this pile of chains you call society,
instead they will fall off of me
as I become the woman I want to be.

I have risen from the ashes
of which you have cremated me,
but those are not truly mine,
they are merely a distraction, see

I swore to defend myself in times
of harm and hurt,
so it is time for me to recognize your sins
and brush you off

How curt, they say, with no regard
for those remarks they made with our
future in mind but rather than that
the idea that man would control this land.

Upon this mountain, clear and pristine,
I am a queen, so let me be,
I will beckon these shores from sea to sea
and give myself, my all to thee.

Stop.

I want you back, please understand,
I didn't want to let you go.

They told me they'd never give me
a dime or shred of love if I ever
brought up the idea of loving you.

I know it broke your heart and it tore mine
in two because even to this day,

I am still madly in love with you.

I miss the scent of you, the way you'd laugh
softly at my feeble and futile attempts to
crack witty jokes.

I miss the way you'd smile at me,
and tell me it would be ok.

Please take me back, I want you back,
I hope you feel the same way.

To you.

If I am ever gone for long enough
that you begin to question why I left,

I want you to know that it was never your
fault for loving me less.

I was not perfect, or gorgeous, or smart,
I was average, something you believed you
were not.

So if you are wondering why I did what I
did,
know that it is because I knew that you'd
bid.

Saying no matter how unhappy I was, I'd
still stay with you,
but here you are, helpless and destitute.

Consort.

I've been told constantly that I will never
succeed,
for the color of my skin is a constant decree,
that I am not and will never be enough.
I heed your advice,
I bleed, will it suffice?

I've been told that the closest I'll ever
get to becoming what I want,
is a consort to a man who I will support,
obey, and console.

I will be the poor to his rich,
the healthy to his sick,
available to nurse him back to health.

I am the pomp to his valor,
the docility to his honor,
I am side-stepped before I begin
my response,
I am tired, sick, and hungry for it,
the more that I give the more that he has.

The stability of this shore is one
I couldn't want more
so help me God my peers, as well,
as I traverse this unknown.

Capricorn.

Your dreams of avarice have long overtaken any semblance of love you have had for your maiden.

You have made her leave her passion to serve you and do all of your dirty work because you have not wanted to.

You have stolen her soul and hung it to dry with a clothespin given by the thief of the night.

You have wiped the smile clear off of her face,
and smothered goodbye, leaving her with a sour taste.

8 Years.

She is 13 and useless,
14 and hopeless,
15 and broken, shattered by your words.

16 and torture,
17 and a nuisance to your peace,
18 and finally allowed to leave you be for as long as you please.

19 and confused,
20 and she doesn't know what to do,
21 and she finally can do what you did to make her hate you.

Ladylike.

Somewhere someplace
in the middle of the night
where love was banned
and men were always right
there was a goddess, a savior, a queen

She licked her lips and cleared the mist
with the magic of her fingertips
her delicate, mystical
synchronized, criminal hips.

A woman, she was a woman
a powerhouse, mighty woman.

She didn't care what they said
or what they thought,
instead she flipped them off and drove off
far.

Record.

Did I embarrass you?
Was that the reason you left?

You couldn't stand the thought of me
ruining the "reputation" which you evidently
didn't have?

I was too weird, too worthless.
Too fat to stand next to you.

Too natural to fit in with your fake
sense of reality.

To real to give a shit.

You embarrass me, I stick up for you.
You leave me, I am graceful about it.

I let you ruin the reputation I'd spent years
finessing.

You were too demanding, too ruthless.

Too fake to give a shit.

Selfless.

It feels good doing something for myself.

My entire identity is crafted around the idea that I should do what makes others happy.

I know I won't be going to heaven for this.

I have sinned several times, merely doing this now is testament to it.

It's likely I won't see you even at the gates of hell.

So I bid you goodbye.

Goodbye to your useless standards and high expectations.

Goodbye to your hypocritical thinking and overachieving mindset.

Goodbye to your toxicity and hatred for all things different.

Under.

A film of tears coats my eyes,
solemn, uncontrollable, and evil.

Glimmering with sobs unshed over
feelings I never knew I had.

Emotions so volatile I did not
myself trust even the holiest
and purest of humans.

I am digging a hole, six feet deep,
to bury my heart under.

White flowers will line the grave in which it
rests, and the tombstone itself will read

"A reminder of love lost, never found,
for it was not shared with this heart in the
first place."

Hijack.

I am fervent with hope that you
know me well enough to have checked
to see what this is about.

I am certain you know who I'm referencing
but I made sure no one would give you a tip
off.

You have captured my heart, my soul taken
captive, I think only of you.

I know this will never work out between us,
but I hope you'll understand anyway.

Flatline.

I am so scared that
I forget to breathe and I
cannot breathe at all.

SOS

Maybe I want someone to help me.
Maybe I need reassurance that it will be
okay.
Maybe I'm not allowed to ask for help.
Maybe I am weak.
Maybe I am sad, angry, and broken.
Maybe this is all a facade.
Maybe one day in another land,
I will wed my love with a garland of
chrysanthemums.

Toxic.

You were my savior
you fended off the haters
your sweet notes and
infectious smile
made me love you

like a friend, nothing more,
I didn't want to knock on love's door,
but you lit the gasoline and set
a fire called toxic.

But I tried to rescue our
friendship from the flames
but the wrongs were incessant
and we didn't become endgame.

So I left you and the place we met
hoping it would make me okay,
but I ended up more broken than I started.

Jerry.

Her tenacious grip over who I want to be
leaves me helpless and destitute.
Her voice, like honey, is soft and soothes
but inside, I know she is cunning.
Some lucrative business is going on
behind the red barn doors.
I can feel it within me,
I can feel them watching me.
How else would they know my every move?
Demanding reverence and respect
a penetrating glance she wears.
I am scared and hopeless
and filled with despair
for her cronies
are inside my walls..

Monarchy.

They anoint me with holy oil.
Sinful and unholy and greedy.
I want it.
They crown me with plastic jewels.
Shiny and tacky and opulent.
I have it.
They robe me with polyester.
I need it.
They inject me with the villain.
It leaves me.

Lime.

My love is like a lime,
when it is left outside for too long it
hardens and the juice
seeps into its skin.
When I leave you my attention for you
goes into making myself great.

Ambivert.

This time has been particularly difficult on me, perhaps because I thought I would thrive.

I needed friends more than I thought.

I needed to hug them one last time, to tell them goodbye for certain.

I awake my from my dream and realize, that there was no one to which goodbyes could be spoken.

Misogyny.

I want you to tell me that your pain
is the same as mine when in fact it
never can and never will be.

I don't mean to diminish your hurt but the
only way you diminish me is through
attempting to inflame your pain. Which
doesn't exist.

I want you to tell me that you are told to
hide your pain and walk around with shame.

To suck it up, and grow a pair.

You will never live like me, so try respecting
me.

Apology.

Did you forget already?
The happiest day that we'd had?
I'd called you and gotten excited
over our future wedding plans?

I told you a secret and you didn't notice
how my face had changed from those words
before it.
Took a pill to forget all the memories,
and you said you would come and go the
way that you pleased.

Said I was your first love and I knew it,
I knew it wasn't true and you'd say I blew it.
Please forgive me at least for the time being
or maybe we could go right back where we
started.

Gingham.

I know this salt all too well,
table salt, unlike that from the Seychelles.
Vigorously rubbed into brisket
and filets,
but most importantly the way that they say
they have hurt you and slit open
the scab that has tried to heal.
They will detain you by the wrist
and demand that you sit,
when you profusely refuse
they strap you down in their tool
of torture and pain,
they rip open your chains
and slice the wounds open again.
Salt in their hand,
they disregard your command,
instead you feel the grains sinking in.
Screaming out into the open unknown
but unable to be heard at all.

Mica.

Their hopes are blind
their trust is strong
and they are spoken about for a fleeting
moment,
like a song.
They are the workers, with beads
of sweat dripping
each day
with nothing to eat when they go home.
I can't find it in my heart to forgive
or forget.
Their hopes are so high
and their eyes fill with dread
when they know there is nothing at home,
even bread.

Hands.

Her hands are like leather,
coarse like a laborer's,
the turmeric stains in crevices on her
fingertips.
Her palms are worn with age,
indentations traced so many times
there is a disparity in their color.
Her nails are small,
with barely any tips at all,
the layers of *maav*[1] inside them.

---

[1] the Tamil word for dough

7 Days.

Day 1, perfectly fine, jubilant for a while.
Day 2, the opposite, I can't feel my back
again.
Day 3, I'm so worried, about what I'm going
to do next week.
Day 4, there's a knock on the door, and it's
not the one I wanted it to be.
Day 5, I'm sick of my head, I want to go to
bed and leave the world instead.
Day 6, it's been weeks since I've gotten a
proper full night's sleep.
Day 7, I'm ready to part with this pain, and
wake up tomorrow to do it all over again.

Whoever.

You took her dreams and gave him his.
I am enraged as I should be.
You took her soul and made it spin.
I am saddened as I should be.
You took her identity and suppressed it with
his as if it was supposed to stop her.
You are a demon, a monster, who attempted
to make her another version of herself for
him.

Queen.

She is a queen.
She is educated,
beautiful.

She is complete.

She has defied all odds,
broken the glass dome,
and reached the highest
rung of the ladder.

She is grace,
elegance, and dignity.

She looks like me.
She is from the same place as me.

I can be like her,
she has told me.

Final.

I thought it would be done.

I thought I would have fought
for just a little bit longer.

I'm beginning to wonder whether it's
any use fighting at all, for

people just turn a blind eye to your
suffering because
of the bare necessity.

Help me decide if this life is right for me
after all.

Ice.

I can see straight into your eyes
to pick up on your lies and now
I'm so entrenched in them that I forget to
breathe.

I let the dark cloak envelop me with a hug
warmer than you've ever given me.

Goodbye, my friend.
Goodbye, you liar.
Good riddance.

Vote.

18 is the magic year
where I can begin to vote
for the freedom of our country
depends on my secondhand coat.

It is where I get to choose
where right draws lines for wrong
and finally bequeath my childhood
to the scrapbooks in the attic.

It is where I quell any attempts
to stifle this voice I've gained,
for in my deep and withered voice,
wherein there lies no shame.

I can see the future dawn on this
flag of red, white, and blue,
any sense of democracy obliterated,
my words are harmful too.

I have seen the struggle of those
with melanin-rich skin, those who
toiled and labored in the fields
through morning, thick and thin.

We are on the verge of a new awakening,
unpleasant and ugly is it,
for if we do not open our eyes
we will never even see how fit

A leader we will need to have to wave the
banner once more,
of this country we like to call home,
where freedom is sometimes war.

It is not a mirage in the distance,
our destiny looms before us,
the anguish we are facing now,
is nothing but a prelude to this.

We have witnessed an ambush on sacred
ground,
an insurrection at its finest,
yet in our hands lies the power to change,
the power to make, the power to knead

Our stories into our voices into our
movements into our actions,
because our dreams, our lives, the guarantee
of freedom lies in a ballot.

West.

When I began this journey I expected it to
end.

I wanted to leave the load of problems away
at a rest stop far away from my destination.

I ended up stopping at a gas station and
picking up a few more along the way.

I don't know where I am going anymore,
this heat is too sweltering to see.

I cannot feel my back anymore,
my legs are as thin as a tree.

My hair is a lion's mane when it roars,
my skin the color of yellowed parchment.

My eyes are bloodshot and foggy yet clear,
my ears ring with the sound of tears.

Telephone.

You want me to fail I know it
but I am strong, and I won't show it.
You're greedy and cruel and hurtful,
but my words are like a whip, brutal.
I feel your eyes fixate on my skin,
and I remember the places I've been.
You think I'm so nice,
like a doormat to be walked on,
I'll teach you nice,
and lead you, you pig to the slaughter.

48.

We have longed for a while,
stood the test of time
for a leader whom will pick
up the broken pieces of our nation,
and say that "this too will be fixed".

We have hurt for forever,
protested with great fervor,
for a harbinger of peace
and harmony.

As we dance on this day,
filled with joy, the dismay
of those who have shut us out
will echo from the rooftops crowned with
shingles in gray,

a place we can finally call home.

Forgotten.

Don't go, please, I don't want you to leave.
I want you to hold my hand until I need to
go.
You didn't deserve this pain,
this hatred, it's going against the grain.
You have enveloped everyone in a hug of
sorrow one last time.
They say you are "attention seeking" or that
you have read too many teenage novels for
you to understand the real meaning of pain.
Then when you die, it is "how could I have
missed it?"

13.

I am 5, young, and bold,
a sunflower in the classroom, covered head
to toe in mud.
I am 6, emotional and sad,
leaning back in the mirror,
so my hair can be long.
I am 7, impressionable and bubbly, wearing
mismatched pants and shirts, and
accessorizing with bows.
I am 8, rosy and chubby,
crying weekly at elementary angst.
I am 9, tall and plump, "borrowing" mom's
Pashmina scarves, and draping them like
sarees.
I am 10, shy and meek,
my handwriting has become everyone's
envy.
I am 11, sad and tired,
my mirror becomes my best friend.
I am 12, empty and envious,
of those lives that are perfect on paper.
Now I am 13, hopelessly romantic,
but helplessly single.

Ending.

As with any film, it comes to a close.
Whether or not that close is adequate
is up to you to decide.
Each frame was handcrafted,
every shot carefully planned.
The filters and editing make this
truly grand.
Thank you for watching should fill the
screen.
As I bid you goodbye,
for the last time before I leave.

Acknowle dgements

The creation of this book would not be possible without the love and support of my family.

Amma and Appa, you are my world. Thank you for believing in my writing and encouraging me to believe in myself too.

Neha, I know you are not old enough to read yet, but if you sound out these words, know how much I love you.

To my friends- thank you for showing me the definition of a relationship. I have gained a tremendous amount from speaking to you everyday.

To my teachers, past and present- you have shown me the true definition of hard work.

Despite this unprecedented situation, you have continued to make learning in your class a wonderful experience.

I fondly recollect your nurturing, which has helped me grow into the writer that I am today.

To my precious, voracious readers- thank you for taking the time to read this book.

I am humbled and grateful at this opportunity to create a community filled with people who have experienced these feelings with such fervor.

Thank you from the bottom of my heart.

About Nethra.

Nethra fell in love with words before she could fully speak them. Phonetically spelling words, she started her journey of writing at the tender age of four. In writing she found her voice, her paint colors, her brushstrokes, and an insight into life and the things around her. When not actively involved in her coursework, Nethra plays the piano, trains in ballet, and engages in her community by participating in youth-led community service organizations. In her spare time, Nethra enjoys singing, learning new languages, and performing in musical theatre. *This Impertinent Life* is her debut collection of poetry. Nethra lives in the United States with her family. To learn more, visit Nethra's website.

www.ingramcontent.com/pod-product-compliance
Lightning Source LLC
Chambersburg PA
CBHW020728160726
47993CB00006B/2383